MW01224777

Justice Institute
715 McBride Boulevard
New Westminster, BC   V3L 5T4

$25.95

Aggression Control
Teaching the "Out"

Stephen Mackenzie

DISCARDED

Aggression Control:
Teaching the Out
© 2009 Stephen Mackenzie

Library and Archives Canada
Cataloguing in Publication

Mackenzie, Stephen A. (Stephen
Alexander), 1948-
Aggression control : teaching the out /
Stephen Alexander Mackenzie.

ISBN 978-1-55059-368-6

1. Dogs--Training. 2. Dogs--Behavior.
3. Aggressive behavior in animals.
I. Title.

SF431.M34 2009   636.7'0887
C2009-905471-X

All rights reserved. No part of this book
can be reproduced in any form or by any
means without written permission from
the publisher.

We recognize the support of the
government of Canada through the Book
Publishing Industry Development
Program (BPIDP) for our publishing
program.

We acknowledge the support of the
Alberta Foundation for the Arts for our
publishing program.

SAN 113-0234
ISBN 978-1-55059-368-6

DETSELIG
ENTERPRISES LTD

210 · 1220 Kensington Road NW   *p. 403.283.0900*
Calgary, Alberta T2N 3P5   *f. 403.28.6947*
www.temerondetselig.com   *e. temeron@telusplanet.net*

Dedication

To Rusty: a half Labrador, half Irish Setter who saved a young boy's life by retrieving him out of Lake Samamish, WA in the early 1950s. Rusty is long gone now; but because of him the little boy grew up to write this book.

Acknowledgments

The author is indebted to the following: William Nott, Jr., John Brannon, and Franco Angelini for sharing their personal adaptations of the author's original methods; and John Johnston of Ace K9, Lisa Brannon of Shallow Creek Kennels, and Franco Angelini for providing photographs.

Table of Contents

Preface

The history of working dog training is full of compulsive, and in some cases abusive techniques. When the author started his career, it was common for trainers to rely on pain to teach dogs what was expected of them, and motivation was limited to their love of biting on the one hand and their desire to avoid painful consequences on the other. The idea that aggressive dogs could learn things in pleasant ways was not even considered in most circles. Young trainers were taught that painful techniques were necessary to control strong animals and we all used them because the older, more experienced trainers did and we all wanted to look as much like them as possible. It was not unusual to see people hanging and swinging dogs (off the ground) in obedience and using sharpened pinch (or prong) collars (two around the neck and sometimes another around the belly) and large amounts of electricity to teach the dogs to release the decoy (known as outing) after a bite. Fortunately, the last thirty years have seen a swing towards more pleasant techniques, especially in obedience and search work; but aggression control has been a hold out for the old, unnecessarily harsh methods. Somehow, we think that because aggression is involved, we must continue to use force and pain as major tools for aggression control. This is not true, and never has been. The issue is not whether or not the harsh methods work, but whether or not they are necessary. Operant Conditioning was well defined by B.F. Skinner in 1938, and we have had plenty of time since then to apply its principles to dog training. Trainers working with other potentially dangerous species including lions, tigers, bears, and killer whales have done so, using positive reinforcement to great effect in controlling the animal's aggression. If more pleasant techniques work in these species, they will certainly work in aggressive dogs as well.

In the early 1980s, the author began writing and teaching seminars about the newer techniques for teaching the out as described in this book. The methods were not well received, to say the least. The techniques were generally ridiculed and the author attacked both personally and professionally. He learned to stop speaking of them and only shared them with a few like-minded students. However, interest in these techniques is growing in leaps and bounds now that people are seeing more dogs trained with these methods. Unfortunately, there are no good references for instructors to recommend to their followers. This book is an effort to provide the first written reference for trainers and handlers who wish to move away from the old techniques and improve the reliability of their dog's behavior and the quality of their lives.

Chapter 1
The Yerkes-Dodson Law

Aggression control work requires dogs to be able to think while they are excited. Many of the imported dogs we have been working with lately are having difficulty with this, so a look at the relationship between excitement and cognitive abilities seems to be in order.

In the early 20th century, there were two psychologists named Robert M. Yerkes and John D. Dodson, who began looking at the relationship between emotional arousal and performance. They published a paper in 1908, in which they described what is now known as the Yerkes-Dodson Law, or the "inverted U". As *figure 1.1* shows, they noticed that there is an optimum level of excitement or arousal for any given task. As excitement levels drop or increase from this optimum, performance of the animal decreases. So dogs that start on the left side of the inverted U need to have their excitement levels increased in order to reach good performance, whereas dogs which start on the right side of the curve need to have their excitement levels decreased in order to perform well. All of our decisions need to be made in light of where we think the dog is on the curve and which way our actions will push it. While there are bound to be minor exceptions to every rule, the Yerkes-Dodson Law has been well accepted for a hundred years now, and we should pay attention to it.

The natural excitement levels of the dog are heavily influenced by genetics and early experience. If we did not personally breed and raise the dog, we have had little influence over its natural excitement levels, but we are still responsible for recognizing animals that are too excitable to make good police dogs. We should learn to recognize dogs whose arousal levels are optimum and those whose levels are too high for good performance.

Fig 1.1

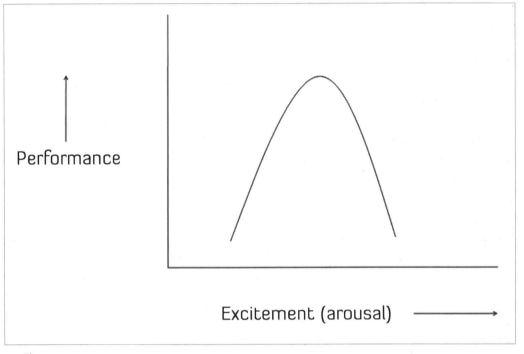

Fig. 1.1

One of the major differences between police service dogs and sport dogs is that police dogs must think well enough to solve problems even when highly excited and under stress. Their ability to release the adversary and return to cover with only a verbal command from the handler is critical for their survival when an ordinary deployment surprisingly turns into a gun battle. More than this, we must never select animals that will be so difficult to control that the handler will be tempted to break cover in a dangerous situation simply because his/her dog is being difficult.

In a tactically difficult situation, there's nothing better than a good dog that thinks well and is controllable, and this is directly linked to the type of dog we select for training in the first place. We must select dogs whose genetics and upbringing place them in the upper left-hand portion of the inverted U, so that when excitement levels increase they will still be capable of good performance. What happens far too often is that we accept dogs into training whose genetics and upbringing place them in the upper right-hand part of the curve. Then, when the procedures and situations involved in training and deployment increase their excitement levels, these dogs are pushed too far to the right on the curve, and their performances suffer terribly. This eventually puts their handlers at risk, all because we made a bad choice about which dogs to take into training.

> We should learn to recognize dogs whose arousal levels are optimum and those whose levels are too high for good performance. One of the major differences between police service dogs and sport dogs is that police dogs must think well enough to solve problems even when highly excited and under stress.

It is time for us to recognize that highly motivated dogs have the ability to focus on the task at hand. Any energy which is not able to be focused is simply wild and uncontrollable, not a sign of "high drive". All too often, wild uncontrollable dogs are being confused for highly motivated dogs, and we actually pay people money for them. Do not blame the vendors for this: when we stop paying money for them, the vendors will stop bringing them to us.

The training and handling procedures we choose will also generate characteristic amounts of arousal or excitement. We must be careful to choose techniques that are appropriate for each individual dog. Dogs which are on the left side of the inverted U will need to have more excitement in the techniques used, whereas those on the right side of the curve will need calm or even dull procedures.

Trainers must constantly adjust their techniques to match the dogs they are training. Years ago, the only dogs available for training had medium excitement levels, which placed them somewhere in the middle of the left side of the curve. Consequently, training techniques were developed to increase their excitement levels. With time, these techniques became standard, and were applied to all dogs indiscriminately. Now that we are getting more imported dogs with higher excitement levels, these old standard techniques are getting us into trouble. We can no longer excite dogs randomly and get away with it. We must develop calmer techniques for teaching these high-end dogs in order to keep them in the top part of the curve and maximize their performance. What the future holds cannot be predicted, except that as the gene pool of our dogs changes, we must make whatever adjustments are necessary to keep them at the proper excitement levels.

Pain creates excitement, and will increase the arousal level of any dog. It is unpleasant excitement, but excitement nonetheless. When we use high levels of pain for teaching aggression control work, we are pushing the dog farther to the right on the curve, ensuring that it can't release and do the correct thing. Once the dog is on the far right hand side of the curve, the only tool we have left is an abusive amount of pain, which will create an "escape reaction" in the dog. This ensures that we will have to keep using far more pain to train the dog than was actually necessary if we had stayed in the optimum part of the curve. This will quickly set up an adversarial relationship between the dog and handler, since we select dogs that do not give in easily to pain. The dogs begin to consider the handlers part of this problem, not part of the solution. Instead of being a team, the dog and handler become competitors. This encourages the dog to cheat on the handler whenever possible, which complicates many aspects of training and will eventually put the handler at risk in dangerous situations.

Pain may be a good enforcer of what has already been learned, but it is not a good tool for initial teaching. With strong aggressive dogs that have high pain tolerances and do not yield to pain easily, we must use pain carefully when teaching or not at all.

Sounds can also increase the arousal level of dogs. Sometimes the sound of gunfire is all that is needed to drive the dog too far to the right on the inverted U. With others, it is the sound of a whip cracking, or a bamboo stick being struck on a sleeve. It can even be the sound of a human screaming rather than speaking in normal tones.

In the early 1980s, the author began using games and favorite toys to reward dogs during aggression control work. This allowed us to avoid the complications of using pain, and is still a successful technique with most dogs, but we are now seeing an interesting development. The gene pool of our dogs is again shifting, and we are seeing more dogs now which were originally bred for ring sport. Such dogs are genetically selected to have an abnormally high interest in objects and toys. This makes it easier to teach them to guard random objects, which is a requirement of that sport. Unfortunately, it is now possible to find dogs which are so obsessed with their toys that merely playing with them creates too much excitement. Fortunately, these dogs are rare, and when you meet one you can simply choose techniques such as the muzzle or the self out to teach the release which do not involve objects or toys. Another approach is to select an object or toy which the dog is less interested in to keep the excitement levels in the proper range.

These are only some examples. You should make your own list of things creating too much excitement based on your own experiences, but the pattern should be clear by now. We must do whatever it takes to keep the dog in the optimum part of the curve. If that means we must select calmer dogs, then we should start doing that. If we have an old-style dog and we must find a more exciting reward, then we must do so. If it means we must stop using so much pain then we must do that. If it means we must use a less exciting reward then that is what we must do. If we must wait longer between repetitions to let an excited dog calm down before we continue training, we must do that. We must do whatever it takes to keep our dogs in the upper part of the inverted U so they can think well enough to learn properly, not only in aggression control, but in everything we do.

Reference:

Yerkes, R.M. and Dodson, J.D. (1908) The relation of strength of stimulus to rapidity of habit-formation. *Journal of Comparative Neurology and Psychology* 18: 459-482.

Aggression Control

Chapter 2
Obedience Sets the Stage

When done correctly, bitework and aggression control are simply extra phases of obedience. The dog is worked in obedience from location to location, from decoy to decoy and occasionally the dog is expected to act aggressively and bite, but the sequence is always followed by a return to control since bitework is always done in the middle of an obedience workout. Dogs quickly adjust to this pattern and realize that no matter how exciting and wild aggression work gets, it is always followed by control. They also learn that this is normal, and nothing to be avoided or resented.

The problem for most dogs is that we separate the phases of obedience and bitework during initial training and have different expectations of them for each phase. During obedience they are required to think in a controlled manner, but during the aggression phase they are allowed to be as wild as they like and we do not require them to come back under control. This causes great difficulty for them in real life situations where there is no separation between phases, and they are expected to combine the lessons of both as though they were humans. This separation of phases in training is a throwback to days when we did not know as much about selecting dogs as we do now. In those days, we ended up with many weak dogs in training, which needed this approach, but such is not the case now.

> The problem for most dogs is that we separate the phases of obedience and bitework during initial training and have different expectations of them for each phase.

The quality of dog that enters training is better today than it has ever been, and in fact it is more common to see dogs that are too wildly aggressive than it is to see weak ones. These better animals are quite capable of understanding that obedience and bitework are the same phase of training, and that the rules for both are exactly the same. It is usually the human handler who has difficulty understanding this.

Time and time again I meet handlers who have dogs with control problems because of the manner in which they handle the dog. For example, if they give the down command during obedience, they expect the dog to down quickly and to assume the correct position and alignment. However, if they give the same command during aggression work, they allow the dog to down in a slower manner or not at all, and if the dog is crooked in alignment the handlers says nothing. After all, the dog is highly excited and distracted, so if it doesn't down that is understandable, and if the dog downs at all that is pretty good. Who cares how he does it?

Well, the dog cares. Dogs are quite capable of learning concepts, and we get so focused on specific actions that many times we fail to pay attention to the concepts we are teaching. What the above handler just taught his dog is that the rules are different in aggression work than they are in obedience. He taught the dog that when aggression is involved, the dog can behave differently than it does in obedience, and the handler will accept that. He also taught the dog that whenever it gets excited it is acceptable for the dog to behave badly. If all this is true for the down, the dog will wonder what else it is true for and will begin testing to find out. Unfortunately, most find out that the rules are different for everything. This discovery produces a lot of dogs with control problems.

So how can we avoid these problems? We can start thinking of aggression control during the very first obedience session. Everything we do should be in preparation for what is to come later. We know that later the dog will be required to act normally in the presence of a decoy in full gear. It will also be expected to obey obedience commands when it is extremely excited, and in particular, it will be expected to release things from its mouth when it is extremely excited. We know that in real life there is no separation between bitework and obedience, they exist in the same time frame. We know that when a dog call becomes a gun fight, a dog that can be recalled from a distance and put in a down under cover has a much higher chance of surviving the situation. Many handlers have a tendency to break cover to gain control of their dog when it refuses commands during tactical situations. These handlers are unwilling to sacrifice their canine partners and expose themselves to greater risk than they would have to if they had a better controlled dog. Control problems often put handlers at risk, as well as the dog.

To prepare the dog for these things we can start with the decoy. There should be a decoy in full protective gear present for most, if not all obedience sessions. He should not act in an aggressive manner or try to cause trouble for the handlers or their dogs. The dog should become accustomed to working calmly and precisely around the decoy. The emphasis should be on how the decoy is acting, not what he is wearing or carrying. This will help prevent dogs from reacting aggressively at a later stage simply because the decoy appears on the field. They will learn that normal behaviors from the decoy require a normal, non aggressive response, and that the rules for obedience when a decoy is present are exactly the same as when he is not. It is better for the dog to learn this first, instead of allowing uncontrolled, wild behavior around decoys, and then trying to punish the dog into controlled behavior later. Good trainers have known for a long time that it is better to teach the acceptable alternative first and then try to eliminate the others than to do it in reverse order. It would make sense to do this in aggression control as well.

Let us take a quick break to establish an important fact. Aggression is simply another form of behavior. It responds to all the things that any other behavior responds to. It is not a mysterious monster that defies the laws of behavioral science. The same laws of learning, reinforcement and punishment that apply to obedience, agility, article search, tracking, trailing, area search and detection work apply to aggression as well. We do not have to treat the dog differently simply because we are dealing with aggression. If we can use tools such as praise, games and toys in the obedience, tracking and detection phases, we can use them effectively in aggression control as well. It is just another form of behavior.

Once the dog is acting normally around the decoy we need to define how much freedom the dog will have in the future. This affects the way the dog will relate to control work later. We need to teach the dog from the very start that when it complies with obedience commands life is fun. There is never a good reason to refuse a command because what it can gain from doing the correct thing is always better than what it will get if it does something else. We need to teach the dog that it is always in the dog's best interest to do as we say. This is a concept and any way we teach it is acceptable, it does not necessarily need to be done through pain and force. What is important is how we define the handler in the dog's mind as we do it. The relationship between the dog and handler is a critical factor later when we begin aggression control work, and it is much better for us if we define the handler as part of the solution instead of part of the problem. Too many people set the handler up in the mind of the dog as someone who takes things away and is part of the problem the dog has to solve, instead of a friend and partner who will help it solve whatever problem it is facing. This adversarial relationship

> Aggression is simply another form of behavior. It responds to all the things that any other behavior responds to. It is not a mysterious monster that defies the laws of behavioral science. ... We do not have to treat the dog differently simply because we are dealing with aggression.

works against us later, when we need the dog to release the decoy and return to our control. Many handlers who have not been established as a friendly leader and partner have great difficulty when the dog begins to fight them mentally during control work. This often begins during obedience due to the way we define the handler. If we are constantly using force and pain, we are teaching the dog that the handler is not really on its side, and that cheating and evading what the handler wants is beneficial for the dog. What we need to teach is that the handler is always offering what the dog will enjoy the most, and there is no need to evade his wishes. Then when we follow this up with the concept that we will never, ever accept disobedience (by always keeping after the dog until we get what we want) we have a complete behavioral package that will serve us well later. Too many people still go straight to pain and force which causes a lot of cheating and competition in the dog later.

> Many handlers who have not been established as a friendly leader and partner have great difficulty when the dog begins to fight them mentally during control work. This often begins during obedience due to the way we define the handler.

Getting back to the idea that there is no separation between obedience and aggression in real life, we should pay some attention to the locations in which we teach obedience. Many times we begin obedience training in an open grassy area which has no resemblance to the areas that we will need the dog to work in later. This is not an evil thing, these areas are simply available and pleasant for the dog. However when we set demanding standards on a football field and lessen our expectations when we move to areas around cars, roads and buildings, we have again taught the dog that obedience is a separate phase and is of secondary importance. We then end up with dogs which ignore commands when they are in or around their car and who are difficult to control in the very locations where we need

21

control the most. Sound familiar? Fortunately, this problem can be alleviated by teaching obedience in and around the dog's vehicle from the very start. Choose safe parking lots or quiet roads but make sure each session has the dog jumping in and out of its vehicle and doing some obedience right inside the car. Have the decoy interacting in a friendly manner during this time, so that the dog learns that it must behave properly around vehicles and decoys. This will pay off later when the dog has to do aggression control for vehicle stops. Be sure to include buildings (inside and outside) and any other location you will expect the dog to show control in. In general, teach obedience in the most realistic locations possible right from the start, and you will be in much better shape when you get to aggression control.

> Some dogs have trouble with control when they hear or see things which they associate with aggression and biting. We can help them retain control by breaking up these associations by teaching neutral responses during obedience.

What we did earlier with the decoy was to teach a neutral reaction to his presence and his equipment. It is important to do this with other things as well. Some dogs have trouble with control when they hear or see things that they associate with aggression and biting. We can help them retain control by breaking up these associations by teaching neutral responses during obedience. The classic example is the sound of gunfire. Tactical experts are clear in their preference of dogs which do not react to either the sight of a firearm in the hands of the handler or the sound of guns. This can be accomplished easily by firing guns from a distance during obedience and demanding the same normal performance as always. Some trainers have had good success having the handler produces a toy or reward every time the dog hears gunfire. With time, the dog begins to check the handler every time it hears a gun, which gives the handler control of the situation. With time, the gun can be moved closer and closer, until the desired proximity is reached. Drills should be developed in which the handler assumes different defensive positions and draws an empty pistol, aims it, and changes magazines. Be sure to include the prone position, since lowering your body is a signal in the dog world to come here, and many dogs will break whatever position you put them in to come over and see what you are doing when they first see you lie down. They need to hold whatever position you put them in without interfering with your shooting ability, regardless of what you are doing.

Eventually, the handler should be able to fire blanks or live rounds at the range without any reaction from his dog. You should not be satisfied until your dogs can do this. Do not get excessive with this; remember that they have sensitive hearing that can be damaged. Do not forget whatever formation you will be using for tactical tracking and building searches. Have the formation move as a unit during obedience, and teach the dog not to react to the back-up officers when they begin firing first. Without this training, most dogs turn on the back-ups in a real situation and take them out without hesitation. When this has happened a few times, no one wants to go with you on high risk tracks, and it gets lonely out there. You should be able to do anything you want with firearms and have the dog react in a neutral manner. It will be a great advantage later when the dog has to show control after it has heard gunfire.

As stated above, this is an area where toys and games have been used quite effectively. Toys have been used for years to teach the neutral response to gunfire. It begins with regular obedience and moves on to drawing and using all the equipment on the handler's belt in all positions including prone. When the dog stays in a calm down during this, it is rewarded with a toy or game. Then gunfire from a small caliber firearm is introduced from a distance. When the dog looks towards the source of the gunfire, a toy is used to refocus the dog on the handler. With time, the dog begins to anticipate the toy, and begins to look to the handler whenever it hears gunfire. Larger caliber firearms are then used from a distance and moved closer and closer to the dog until the dog remains calm and looks to the handler when people are firing right in front of it.

After the dog bites someone in a fight and the human complies, the dog will be commanded to release them. The dog will then be expected to follow certain procedures, such as lying down and guarding the suspect, returning immediately to the handler, or some combination of both. These procedures should be thoroughly taught during obedience, with no biting by the dog until they are almost second nature. If the dog will later be asked to guard suspects during arrest and handcuffing procedures, it will help to introduce these during obedience also. It is often a sound tactical decision for the handler to remain under cover at a distance from the dog and suspect and control the situation with verbal commands. They frequently have the suspect face away from them and walk backwards towards them under the watchful eye of the dog, which remains in a down. As the suspect gets too far away from the dog, he is stopped, and the dog is called towards the handler. When it reaches the location of the suspect, it is put in another down, and the suspect is commanded to continue his backing towards the handler. This keeps the handler under cover, while the dog is always close enough to prevent the suspect from escaping. Any procedures of this nature, whether it is tactical leapfrogging with back-up officers or building entry with a tactical team, should be taught in obedience first.

Certain verbal commands for people are worth including at this point. When you issue a verbal challenge to a person later, you will need to hear what they are saying back to you. You do not need a dog that is barking uncontrollably and keeping you from hearing what is going on. This is particularly true in building searches. For weeks before they are used during aggression work, all challenges and warnings that you want a neutral response to should be used in obedience at full volume when there is nothing associated with them and the dog is expected to pay attention to its obedience. Remember that calmness and excitement are behaviors, they can be rewarded just like anything else.

Many trainers have discovered the value of using toys and games as rewards during obedience, tracking, and detection work. They have noticed higher levels of performance when they use these motivators. They have found that when they have dogs that are suitable for the work, trainers can use toys and games during obedience and still get top performance during aggression work. The dogs can track for toys and still bite adversaries at the end of high risk tracks and perform as well as ever during aggression work. The dogs can search intensely for their toy during the detection phases and still show their usual enthusiasm for aggression work.

This approach has not been without controversy. When civilian obedience trainers first began using toys and games to improve performance, there was concern that the dogs involved would break obedience when they encountered children playing with the dog's favorite toy on the street. The trainers discovered that dogs had individual reactions to this temptation, but that all good dogs could be trained to ignore toys the same way that food reward dogs were trained to ignore hot dogs that were dropped by children. It was simply another distraction that could be trained against. This training became known as "proofing" the dog against the food or the toys. This approach has been so successful that trainers currently have no doubts about the practical efficiency of using toys during obedience training provided the dogs are properly "proofed" against the toys as part of the process. Their dogs are completely reliable in the real world.

When tracking trainers began to use toys as the reward at the end of the track, and even as multiple rewards left along the track there was concern that the dogs would only be looking for toys at the end of their tracks, and would not engage an adversary should the need arise. What these trainers discovered was that if an adversary was occasionally placed at the end of a track, dogs that already had an enjoyment for aggression work were more than willing to ignore toys on the track to engage a human. It has become clear that dogs which are suitable for the work will work hard to obtain toys and games, but can be effectively "proofed" against the distraction of toys and games when the handler says it is time to work. It has also become clear that suitable dogs will choose toys and games when such are the only rewards available, but will choose the excitement of a good fight over them whenever possible. In general, toys and games have increased the motivational levels of many dogs in different phases of training, and have not interfered with the aggressive potential of dogs that are suitable for the work and who have good trainers who know how to balance them properly. Again, aggression is simply a behavior. It does not defy the laws of science, and we do not have to treat our dogs differently in later phases simply because we are dealing with aggression.

> In general, toys and games have increased the motivational levels of many dogs in different phases of training, and have not interfered with the aggressive potential of dogs that are suitable for the work and that have good trainers who know how to balance them properly.

An interesting use of obedience to prepare the dog for aggression control is to teach it to release a toy before we ask it to release anything else (like a decoy) later when it is more excited. It is not clear when this technique was first used, but it has been around for a very long time. It has several advantages worth considering. It allows the handler to introduce excitement gradually (proper game playing is a form of excitement), never increasing it quite enough to make the dog lose control, but building the dog's tolerance for it every session. During this process, the dog is always required to come back under control, and the rules of obedience remain the same even when the dog is getting more and more excited. As we discussed earlier, this is an important concept to teach dogs which will have to master aggression control later. This technique allows us to teach it independently of aggression and bitework, so that if problems arise we can work on them without having any direct effect on the quality of the dog's aggression. The dog soon learns that releasing things from the mouth is simply a normal part of obedience, the rules of which never change. Like everything else in obedience, the handler will never accept disobedience or sloppy behavior regardless of the location or circumstance (remember that we are doing obedience around decoys in full equipment, around cars and in locations where we will do tactical work later) and there is no need to evade the command, since good things that the dog will enjoy always follow the procedure.

This is a good time to teach another concept, namely that when the handler tells the dog to release something from its mouth, he is not an adversary who is merely taking something away. He will insure that the dog either gets the object back fairly quickly, or he will provide another toy which is just as much fun, or he will find a way to change the game into something else which is almost as much fun as the original. The handler will insure that the dog never has to give up what is in its mouth for nothing. He is on the dog's side. In the dog's mind he is part of the solution, not part of the problem. This cooperative relationship helps reduce the problem of dogs cheating and evading commands later when we ask them to

The handler will insure that the dog never has to give up what is in its mouth for nothing. He is on the dog's side. In the dog's mind he is part of the solution, not part of the problem. This cooperative relationship helps reduce the problem of dogs cheating and evading commands later when we ask them to release the most exciting thing of all, a human being.

release the most exciting thing of all, a human being. What it will get for releasing the human may not be quite as exciting as the fight itself, but it will be a close second, and the dog will know it will never be asked to give up something for nothing, or merely to avoid pain. When the handler is involved, disobedience or sloppiness will never be accepted, but there will always be something in it for the dog. Animals that think this way are much easier to work with in aggression control.

Obedience is not considered complete until the dog is proofed off all toys and games to the point that when it is working it is not tempted to accept them from anyone but the handler. If you are not experienced in this, a good obedience trainer can help. If proofing is not completed there will be trouble later when these items are used for reinforcement of good behavior. If proofing is not maintained, you will also have trouble. To reduce the need for pain compliance, you must incorporate a complete system of training where the dog is always prepared for what comes next. If you begin preparing it during obedience for the use of toys and games later you will increase the quality of the dog's life immeasurably and training will be smooth and pleasurable for both dog and human. If you take shortcuts or fail to maintain proofing, you will get all the trouble you can imagine.

Chapter 3
The Self Out

Originally called the Combined Method, the self out does not require any toys or game playing in order to be effective. Trainers who are worried about their dogs looking for toys instead of concentrating on the adversary can use this method, and their dogs will never even see a toy.

Preparation for this technique includes everything discussed in *Chapter 2* on obedience, so all of you who skipped the second chapter go back and read it now before you go any farther. *Chapter 2* was not written so that you could skip it. It was written because the material in it directly affects the teaching of control during aggression work. Obedience really does set the stage.

The self out relies on muscle physiology and the trainer's ability to read the dog. Muscles produce lactic acid, or lactate when they contract. When the lactic acid reaches a certain concentration, muscles get sore, fatigue, and eventually stop working. This is a physiological fact, and cannot be changed. The muscles in the dog's jaw are subject to this, just like any others. So no matter how tough the dog, if it has to bite hard to hold onto something, it will eventually fatigue chemically, and be forced to release the object. Dogs do not seem to enjoy this experience any more than human athletes enjoy fatigue and exhaustion. When they have suffered through it a few times, they seek ways to avoid it. So this technique involves working the dog as we normally would in order to get it to bite, and then keeping it on the bite as long as it can physically hold on. During this time, we work on the bite and then we calm down and say nothing, or we gently encourage the dog since it is doing exactly what we told it to do. We simply wait for the fatigue to set in, at which time the dog will release by itself. We allow the aggression to extinguish. During the fatigue phase, the quality of the bite may suffer, but this is only due to the fatigue and does not cause problems with the bite later. As the dog releases on its own, we speak the release command (hopefully already taught to the dog for releasing its favorite toy during obedience, see *Chapter 2*) and tell the dog what a good dog it is. We then have a dog that wants to bite, but after a short period of biting is motivated to avoid the long road to fatigue. In other words, we have a dog that initially wants to bite, but after a short time actually wants to release. All we have to do is to hold off our release command until the dog is going to release anyway, and we are guaranteed compliance with no resistance from the dog and without the necessity for harsh treatment. When this is done repeatedly, the dog associates the command with the action, and eventually, if we can read when the dog is about to release on its own, we can precede the action with the command and the dog soon releases on command. When done correctly, the dog begins to release sooner and sooner, probably due to a desire to avoid the fatigue. Soon, the dog releases on command in a normal time frame.

> This method has the major advantage of allowing us to teach by rewarding good behavior instead of punishing bad behavior.

It is important to believe this, because some dogs hold on a very long time in the beginning of the process. Many trainers lose patience and stop using the technique, thinking it doesn't work. It will work if you believe in it, have enough patience and can read the dog properly. This method has the major advantage of allowing us to teach by rewarding good behavior instead of punishing bad behavior. It has long been known that punishment is only a temporary tool and that what is learned through it will have to be re-taught in a short amount of time. That is why dogs taught through punishment need to be "cleaned up" on a regular basis, often at short time intervals. However, many of our really tough dogs are also quite smart and learn quickly with positive reinforcement. The self out simply waits for the dog to do what we want, gives the command at the same time and praises the dog for complying when it was going to do it anyway. The dog can please the handler and avoid the fatigue at the same time. The handler is not taking away anything that the dog still wants, so with this procedure no competition develops between the dog and handler. Not only do we get the behavior we want but we maintain the good relationship between the two. The handler is helping the dog avoid the bad alternative, so there is no reason for the dog to resent anything or cheat on him.

Since the dog will always release eventually, the trainer is free to work on anything else he chooses. The quality of the bite can be emphasized during the same time frame as the release. Fullness and power can be developed with every bite and the dog will still release. The bite will get better and better at the same time that the release is improving, and you can begin working on the release as soon as you begin working on the bite. Compared to other techniques, this increases the number of repetitions you get on the release during the same amount of time. More repetitions are usually a good thing. These advantages make the self out a good choice for green dogs and in fact it works best with inexperienced dogs which have no bad memories of aggression control work. In the dog's mind the release becomes a natural part of every bite so it does not become a big issue or something worth arguing about with the handler.

While the self out is at its best with green, untrained dogs, it is also very effective with experienced animals which have developed bad behaviors. For instance, some dogs are so tough that they can refuse to release the decoy even under the most severe punishments. The more severe the punishment, the more they scream and hang on, biting even harder in most cases. These are cases where the self out can help. Some of these dogs have a genetic predisposition to what is known as pain induced aggression. These dogs react to pain aggressively, and the more pain they feel, the higher their aggression levels become. When we use physical pain on them in the form of punishments, all we have done is to guarantee that their aggression levels will increase instead of decreasing and that they will bite even harder than before. This prevents the dog from releasing even if it wants to. The self out avoids this complication completely, since it does not use punishment or pain to teach. Other dogs have a genetic predisposition for what is known as redirected aggression. This affects the direction in which the aggression will be expressed. When we punish them for not releasing they would like to bite the handler for interfering, but the rules of the dog world say they cannot express aggression towards an upper ranking member of the pack. They can only show serious aggression to lower ranking pack members. All the aggression they would like to use to compete with the handler is redirected from the upper ranking handler to the only lower ranking animal available – the decoy. The result will be that again, the dog will bite harder instead of releasing. The self out avoids all this by not using punishment.

Dogs that have learned to compete with the handler and those who feel that they are dominant over the handler often refuse to release because they don't want to give anything up to the handler. Using the self out, the handler only encourages the dog to bite, he/she never tries to take anything away from the dog, so there is nothing for the two to fight about. Some dogs cannot handle excitement well. For some this is a temporary stage that they go through and they eventually work out of it, while others are like this their entire career, which limits their usefulness in many circumstances. For these dogs, the bite alone is so stimulating that anything else such as punishment or game playing pushes them over the edge mentally, and they refuse to release. They are usually too excited to think clearly, and end up on the far right-hand side of the inverted U (see *Chapter 1* on the Yerkes-Dodson law). The self out allows the handler and decoy to quietly calm the dog and keep the excitement levels at a minimum. This allows the dog to remain clear in its thinking which often results in a good release which can be rewarded. Many times the dogs learn to handle more excitement as they mature and the good release remains. Some dogs get frantic on the bite due to the misuse of compulsive techniques by past trainers. They get tense as the handler approaches, even trying to spin the decoy to get away from the punishment they are certain is coming. In the dog's mind the handler is part of the problem and needs to be avoided. The self out allows you to let the handler stand back and not stress the dog while the release gets better and better. It often improves the relationship between the handler and dog (see *figure 3.9*).

The self out allows the handler and decoy to quietly calm the dog and keep the excitement levels at a minimum. This allows the dog to remain clear in its thinking which often results in a good release which can be rewarded. Many times the dogs learn to handle more excitement as they mature and the good release remains.

We are seeing more and more dogs with extremely high pain thresholds these days. The compulsive techniques developed in the past were effective on animals with average pain thresholds, but are proving to be less effective on many of the dogs we see now. The compulsive techniques were based on what behaviorists call an "escape reaction". This is a response to an overwhelming stimulus. This stimulus is so severe that the animal feels it must stop whatever it is doing and try to escape from it. The old techniques relied on the fact that when a dog refused to release, an extremely painful punishment would cause the dog to stop whatever it was doing (in this case biting) to escape from the pain. This resulted in the dog releasing. It was effective because most dogs had regular or low pain thresholds. These techniques are not working on many of today's dogs because the dog's pain tolerances are so high (meaning they can tolerate so much pain) that it is difficult to apply enough pain to create an escape reaction. This forces trainers to use what many people feel are abusive techniques in desperate attempts to gain control. These attempts are not only difficult, they are unnecessary.

> The self out does not require an escape reaction. It is therefore independent of an animal's pain threshold and can be adapted to work well on all dogs. It doesn't need pain to be effective.

The self out does not require an escape reaction. It therefore is independent of an animal's pain threshold, and can be adapted to work well on all dogs. It doesn't need pain to be effective.

There is an interesting phenomenon involved with using the self out that should be mentioned. When the decoy stops rewarding the dog with fighting and movement, the aggression begins to decrease. Allowing a behavior to decrease and disappear like this is often referred to as the extinction of a behavior. Whenever extinction is used as a behavioral tool we expect to see what is known as an "extinction burst". The behavior, which has been declining for some time, spikes again and becomes strong, as though there has been no improvement (see *figure 3.1*). This is a temporary change and if the extinction is continued the behavior declines again, continues its downward trend and disappears. The problem is that trainers who don't understand extinction bursts get discouraged when they see the behavior "returning" and think that the technique is not working. Many give up at this point, thinking that they have wasted their time, when in fact extinction bursts are normal and expected. They are actually a sign that the extinction process is working.

Flexibility is another advantage of the self out. Trainers who wish to avoid toys and game playing can do so and still get good releases

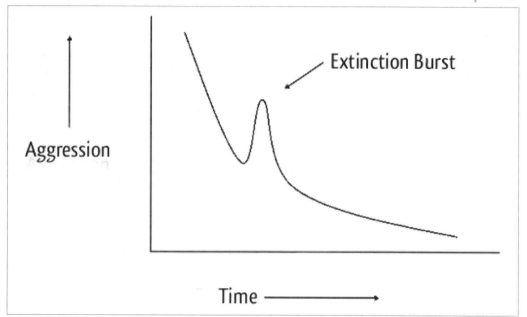

Fig 3.1

Figure 3.1 · An extinction burst is often seen when using the self out.

without relying on punishment. Trainers who wish to maximize the reward give the dog a second bite (avoiding the use of toys) or wait until the dog releases and then introduce its favorite toy, which encourages the dog to release sooner and significantly cuts down the overall training time. This was actually when the author first experimented with toys in an attempt to save decoy's backs when the dog held on for a long time. He then discovered that most dogs responded well to the toys alone, which has become a more popular approach (see *chapter 5*). Sleeve drops can be used although the self out was originally developed for styles which avoid the sleeve drop. It works well either way (waiting for the dog to release a dropped sleeve is another form of self out). Any style of bite building can be used with it. It works well on external sleeves (see *figure 3.2*), hidden sleeves, muzzles, bite suits and on prone suspects (see *figures 3.3, 3.4 and 3.5*). Although the author originated and pioneered the self out,

Fig 3.2

Fig 3.2 · The author's students using the self-out with an external sleeve: summer, 1981.

a nice adaptation of it that used by Franco Angelini, who quickly realized that having the decoy lay prone is a good way to reduce the significant strain on his/her back. It also increases the reward for the dog. If the dog has been working in social aggression (what trainers refer to as the fight drive) the reward for this behavior is to see submission in the opponent.

The biological function of social aggression is to create and maintain social hierarchies, or pecking orders. A dog which is operating in this type of aggression is fighting to see these signals of submission from its opponent, and feels rewarded when it does. Experienced decoys have long known that one of the ways to reward social aggression is to suddenly start working the dog in predatory

Fig 3.3

Fig. 3.3 · Dog takes a good bite.

aggression, since the signals that trigger predatory aggression also signal the submission the dog was fighting to get when it was in social aggression.

To put this more simply, having the decoy fall down does two things at the same time: it rewards social aggression (the fight drive) and both stimulates and rewards predatory aggression (the prey drive). So whichever type of aggression you have been working the dog in, having the decoy lay prone at the end of the bite rewards the dog. The dog feels satisfied, having fulfilled the purpose of the aggression, and is more willing to give up the decoy. Consequently, having the decoy lay prone after the dog bites well is a good way to reward social and predatory aggression. This makes using the self out on a prone decoy very useful in a number of situations

Fig 3.4

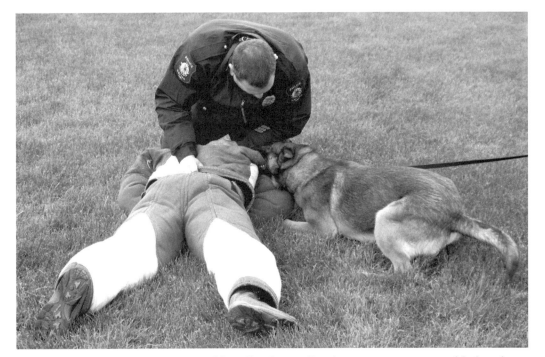

Fig 3.4 · Decoy goes prone and handler immediately moves to protect his head. Dog is allowed to continue biting.

(see *figures 3.6, 3.7, 3.8* and *3.9*). Creative trainers will find many ways to combine it with their favorite routines.

There is also flexibility with regard to the punishment described earlier. If the self out does not rely on punishment, does that mean that you must never use it when training the self out? No. No method will ever be perfect for all dogs without adjustment. Animals are all unique, and we need to adjust to their different personalities if we are to train them well. While the self out can be adjusted to suit any dog there are a small number of them that learn the release well and then just stop doing it. At this point, when we have taught in a positive manner and we are sure that the dog understands how to do it correctly, we may have to apply a reasonable punishment. When this

Fig 3.5

Fig 3.5 · When it has fatigued, the dog releases by itself. Note the calm attitude and lack of competition between dog and handler.

is done in a reasonable manner the dog returns to its former performance level and the relationship between the handler and dog is unharmed. This is why the technique was originally called the Combined Method. It allows us to teach with inducive methods but occasionally combine this with punishment. If you have taught the release correctly you won't have to do this often and the severity of the punishment will be much less than if you had used compulsive methods. Looking at its efficiency on different types of dogs and the variety of choices it gives the trainer, the self out is a valuable tool that is well worth remembering.

Fig 3.6

Fig 3.6 · Prone decoy on a front bite.

CASE EXAMPLE: Max (not his real name) was a young male German Shepherd Dog who had worked for a large inner city K9 unit for several years before his handler brought him to a state wide training workshop. He had numerous solid street bites to his credit, and had a reputation of being a good dog to have around in a dangerous situation. When it came time to work on aggression control, the handler announced that he really only had one problem; namely that Max had never released a decoy voluntarily, even in basic school. They had tried pinch collars, double pinch collars, sharpened pinch collars, and even electricity with no success; when Max realized there was a correction coming he would stiffen his neck, scream, and bite harder no matter what happened. He would spin the decoy around to evade the handler whenever possible, and would cheat and compete with the handler whenever possible to avoid having to release.

Fig 3.7 · Dog noticing handler.

When questioned about Max's other problems, the handler described a very compliant, reasonable dog who was apparently easy to work with in everything else except aggression control. The dog performed well in obedience, tracked well, did article search, building search, area search, and everything else he was asked to do well; he simply would not release the bad guy voluntarily. The handler had adapted his handling style to this, and resigned himself to the fact that his dog would never out. This is an important pattern to watch for; bad dogs, or dogs that are unsuitable for the work, are bad at several things, not just the out. If a dog is suitable for the work, and does everything else well, it will certainly release the decoy if we set it up properly and use appropriate techniques. When a dog performs well at everything else and is only a problem when it is time to out, we are doing something wrong and the situation can be improved. Max seemed to

Fig 3.8

Fig 3.8 · Relaxed dog receiving praise from the handler after release.

be a classic example of this, and we decided to try the self out to see if it would help. As expected, Max hit hard and bit well on the first bite, holding on a long time before he decided to release. If memory serves, it was a full twenty-five minutes before Max released on the first bite, but at the end he was tired and his jaw muscles were fatigued. He was immediately sent back to bite again, which he did. He only held on for about ten minutes the second time, and only for five minutes on the third bite. After a short break to catch his breath and cool down, he got another set of three bites, and the time he was willing to hold on got shorter and shorter. Throughout the process, the handler continued to praise Max for biting and also for releasing, so the dog understood that both things were good. Soon, Max was not interested in hanging on to decoys at all (his jaws were too fatigued), and the

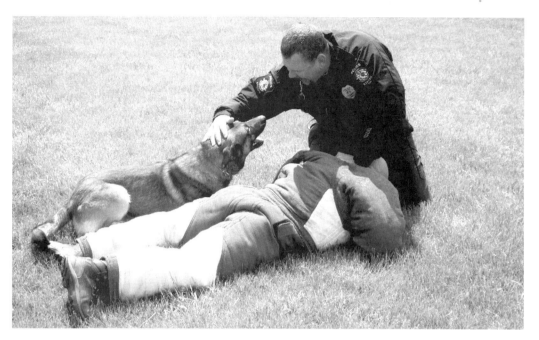

Fig 3.9

Fig 3.9 · The self out can improve the relationship between dog and handler. The dog has no need to cheat on or compete with the handler.

handler started giving the out command just before the dog would have released anyway. When the dog released, the handler gave him maximum praise, and Max, who had never really wanted to be a problem, began to learn that releasing the decoy was actually to his benefit, and was another way to please his handler while still getting to bite things. It doesn't always work this fast, but in a few hours Max was outing normally. The self out allowed us to reward good behavior without needing to use punishment, which he had always fought against. It took away the need for Max to compete with his handler and ushered in a new era of cooperation, forever changing their relationship.

Aggression Control

Chapter 4
The Muzzle

One of the big problems in teaching aggression control comes when the dog already has its teeth in the decoy and refuses to release. Another is when the dog is tempted to cheat just a little bit in order to get its teeth into the decoy. Most of our problems teaching the out centre around the dog getting its teeth into the decoy or already having its teeth in him/her. If we remove the dog's teeth from the picture, we would take away its major tool for resisting and cheating on us. This is exactly what the muzzle does. It allows us to teach without the fear of the dog latching onto the decoy and disrupting training by holding on for the next ten or twenty minutes. A good general rule in dog training is that when the teeth are part of the problem, the muzzle may be part of the solution.

Proper preparation is essential for any type of muzzle work. Go back and read *Chapter 2* again and make sure you are doing all these things in muzzle. Remember that it is not sufficient for the dog to merely accept it; the dog must be so comfortable with the muzzle that it focuses through it mentally and almost forgets about it. The dog's mind must be on the environment and what it is doing, not the muzzle. If it cannot play games like soccer with you without trying to get the muzzle off, it is not ready yet. Keep working until the dog will do perfect obedience and play any game you like without paying any attention to the muzzle.

The drawback to this technique is that it must be used in conjunction with a good muzzle attack to be most effective. You therefore need a decoy who is skilled in muzzle work and not all decoys are good at this kind of work. Once you have such a decoy, you simply end each attack with the release command (which should have been taught on toys without the muzzle during non-muzzle obedience sessions, see *Chapter 2*). If the dog does not cease fighting, you step in and gently yet firmly pull the dog off and place it in whatever position you want it to assume after releasing (usually a down or sit). When it stops fighting you, you praise and reward it. The reward can be anything you can physically arrange, including games and toys, if you can play them in the muzzle or if you can remove the muzzle that quickly. It would be best to keep the dog on leash if you remove the muzzle, since we do not want the dog to be free enough to run back to the decoy and bite him/her. For this reason, most people keep the muzzle on and simply praise the dog and make a big fuss over it to reward it. However, that does not mean you can't be creative and play the dog's favorite game from muzzle obedience or something else the dog would enjoy. There is good flexibility here to adjust the technique to suit different philosophies and techniques.

> A good general rule in dog training is that when the teeth are part of the problem, the muzzle may be part of the solution.

Several repetitions of this sort give even the toughest dogs a chance to learn what is expected of them. If it is done well, most dogs will comply willingly since there is no pain induced aggression created by painful punishments to make it difficult for the dog to comply. There is also no chance of that aggression being redirected into the decoy. The handler is helping the dog succeed, so no competition or resentment develops if the rewards are sufficient in the dog's mind. Care must be taken with dogs which have excitability problems. Few things in a dog's life are as exciting as a good muzzle workout, so the decoy will have to be almost boring in order to control excitement levels in high-end dogs, but at least when they have difficulties they cannot latch on to the decoy and hang on for long periods of time.

Dogs that have suffered severe punishments with a previous trainer may be tense at first when the handler approaches, and they may still try to cheat by moving around the decoy to get away from the handler. However, they cannot delay training by hanging on to the decoy with their teeth and this allows the handler to gently remove and reward

> The dog's mind must be on the environment and what it is doing, not the muzzle. If it cannot play games like soccer with you without trying to get the muzzle off, it is not ready yet.

them for whatever good behavior they exhibit. With time, the dogs learn that things are different with this handler and they need not fear his/her approach. The cheating and competition should begin to decrease at this point. Cheating dogs can still present a problem, though. It is very clear to them when the muzzle in on and when it is off. Some dogs behave perfectly when the muzzle is on, because they know there is no chance of getting a bite, but cheat when the muzzle is off. This does not usually happen when the dog is properly trained in muzzle from the start, but an experienced dog that has already learned to cheat can be more difficult to work with, and may take many repetitions to work through the problem. Dogs with high pain thresholds have no complications with this approach (since it does not rely on pain) and usually learn well in muzzle.

The muzzle can be used by itself or in conjunction with other protective equipment. Some dogs refuse to release anything at any time and certainly the muzzle is beneficial for them; but it is also useful for dogs which simply have too much focus on the sleeve or the bite suit. These "sleeve happy" dogs often release with no problem in real situations on the street, but are so stimulated by the sight of equipment in training that they refuse to comply when the decoy is wearing equipment of any kind. It can be very difficult to get such dogs certified, since most certification tests require the dog to release a decoy wearing some kind of protective equipment. If the decoy sheds equipment, some of these dogs will ignore the decoy and pick up the shed equipment and thrash it. Usually, these dogs have not been set up properly for aggression control during the obedience phase as described in *Chapter 2*, so this needs to be examined but the muzzle is also useful. Working this type of dog in a muzzle when the decoy is fully suited offers trainers and handlers a chance to reward good behavior without having to punish bad behavior. Since the muzzle prevents the dog from behaving badly by hanging on with its teeth, it is easier to help it do the correct thing and gain its reward even when the decoy is wearing tempting equipment, which will eventually lead to better performance (see *Figures 4.1* and *4.2*). The dog can also be encouraged to ignore shed equipment and stay focused on the decoy, and we should not be content until our dog will out properly off a decoy who has shed a jacket or sleeve and stay focused on the decoy, not the equipment (see *Figures 4.3, 4.4, 4.5, 4.6* and *4.7*).

As with other methods, some dogs learn a behavior well and then just stop doing it correctly. At this point a reasonable punishment will have to be applied but this should not be needed often, and the severity should not be great. If severe punishments are needed frequently, you are doing something wrong; go back and check what you are doing.

Fig 4.1

Fig 4.1 · Muzzled dog engaging decoy. *Photo by Lisa Brannon.*

Fig 4.6

Fig 4.2 · Unable to hang on, the dog outs properly. *Photo by Lisa Brannon.*

Fig 4.3

Fig 4.3 · Decoy shedding Jacket on muzzled dog.
Photo by Lisa Brannon.

Fig 4.6

Fig 4.4 · The dog ignores the jacket, outs properly, and stays focused on the man. *Photo by Lisa Brannon.*

Fig 4.5

Fig 4.5 · Still ignoring the jacket, the dog re-engages the decoy.
Photo by Lisa Brannon.

Fig 4.6

Fig 4.6, left ·
Again the dog
outs properly
without
focusing
on the
equipment.

Fig 4.7, below ·
Another look
at the Focus
of the dog.

*Photos by
Lisa Brannon*

Fig 4.7

Chapter 5
Toys and Games

$\mathbf{M}$any trainers have found playing with the dog's favorite toy to be beneficial as a reward and motivator in obedience, agility, article search, building search, area search, tracking, trailing, and detection work, and in the early 1980s the author started using them for teaching aggression control as well. Properly selected dogs which are mentally suitable for the work have shown time and time again that they can learn control through the use of toys and still ignore them to fight a human adversary when given the chance.

Preparation for this style of training includes proper obedience work as described in *Chapter 2*, so go back and make sure you have completed everything mentioned there. In particular, be certain the dog is solid on the behaviors you want after it releases or terminates the attack. Many dogs are tempted to re-bite after they release because they don't know what to do next and are left hanging around with nothing to do. It is a big advantage for them to have a solid idea of what comes next before they get into release training. This utilizes what behaviorists refer to as "chaining", where behaviors are linked together but taught in reverse order so the dog always knows how to succeed in what comes next. The dogs should also be solid at releasing toys (especially tug toys) from their mouths even when they are excited.

When the dog can be placed in front of the decoy and do all the things we want it to do after the bite and release, we can ask it to release its toy before doing all that. It is important for the dog to understand that when it releases, it will get a reward that it really likes and that it is not giving up something for nothing. It either gets the same toy back relatively soon, or it gets a different toy or a different game but it always gets something of high value, not just a little pat on the head. When it can release its toy willingly, trust its handler to provide something else that is just as much fun as the original toy, and follow instructions properly, we can finally add biting the human. Most dogs will have no difficulty with this if you are using a command they already know and they anticipate a good reward when they comply.

> Properly selected dogs which are mentally suitable for the work have shown time and time again that they can learn control through the use of toys and still ignore them to fight a human adversary when given the chance.

Many dogs respond well to an exciting game of tug of war. Others have obsessions for other toys or games, and this is the time to use them. If from day one the dogs have been expected to behave properly around decoys and the rules of obedience have never changed no matter what the location or circumstance, your efforts will really pay off now. Be certain that your decoy does not overly excite the dog, and make sure it has enough time to think clearly before you ask for the release. If you have not taught a release command for the toy, you can use some other obedience command such as "down" so that the dog understands what is expected of it. Proofing off the toys can be accomplished later by having the decoy toss toys and immediately attempt to escape or attack the dog and handler. Other people can throw toys into the situation just before the decoy attacks. The dog will soon learn to keep its attention on the decoy. This will not cause much difficulty if the dog was properly proofed off of toys in obedience. The dog will soon learn to ignore all toys except those offered by the handler.

There are several advantages to this approach. It is highly efficient but more than that it maintains or improves the relationship between the handler and the dog. The handler is not expecting the dog to give up all its fun just to show control, there is always something good in it for the dog. There is no reason for the dog to cheat or avoid the handler's control.

There is great flexibility with this technique. It can be done with external sleeves, hidden sleeves, bite suits or in muzzle (as long as the dog enjoys games in the muzzle). It can be done by using a dropped sleeve as the toy or without dropping sleeves at all. It can be done by teaching the release of its toy first as described above, or

> Practitioners of this technique frequently mention the advantages of breaking complex behaviors down into small components and teaching each separately.

without such preparation. It has worked well both ways, depending upon the dog involved. Practitioners of this technique frequently mention the advantages of breaking complex behaviors down into small components and teaching each separately. Referred to as modular training, this idea has been well known and accepted for many years under a different name. Behaviorists refer to this concept as "chaining" and have been practicing it for a long time.

In chaining, a complex behavior is broken down into individual components much like the links in a chain. Each component is taught separately, and when all have been learned properly they are put together, much like connecting the links in a chain, hence the name "chaining". Any problems are diagnosed and dealt with individually as part of a particular link. What is interesting about chaining is that it works more effectively if the links are put together in a particular order. The individual behaviors are listed in chronological order according to what the dog must do first, second, third, and so on. When the list is complete, the behaviors are taught in reverse order so that the last behavior is taught first, the next-to-last behavior is taught second, the behavior before that is taught third and so on until all the behaviors have been taught, but in reverse order. In this way no matter what is being taught the dog always knows what comes next and knows how to succeed in the next task, so it is never running ahead into the unknown (which makes them insecure). Instead they are constantly proceeding to a task at which they already know how to succeed. This builds their confidence in themselves and their trust in the handler as someone who's never confusing and with whom they always succeed. In addition to improving the relationship between the handler and the dog, chaining seems to increase the speed of learning and how long the dog remembers the complex behavior. So whether we call it modular training or chaining it is worth our while to keep the concept in mind.

Another concept worth remembering is to proof against the patterns we may have used to teach a behavior. We want to break up patterns in the environment so they will not control the dog. For instance, in *Chapter 2* we mentioned the need to have the fully suited decoy around during obedience so his or her presence does not set a pattern that produces aggressive behavior by itself. We want the behavior of the decoy to create aggression, not his or her presence or the clothes and equipment he or she wears. Failure to separate the decoy from the actions that justify aggression produces dogs that become aggressive as soon as the decoy walks onto the field. This will cause problems later when it is time to teach aggression control. To be tactically sound, a dog must relate to the actions of the decoy and the commands of the handler; nothing else should control it. This is the basis of what trainers call "conflict training", where they do things in different ways to break up any patterns they may have set in the dog's mind that may limit the dog's ability to respond properly to unpredictable circumstances. When they are successful the commands of the handler and the actions of the decoy have what behaviorists refer to as "stimulus control", where nothing else controls the dog's behavior. Examples of things to proof against would include equipment, the presence or absence of particular people, the presence of other dogs, different locations, positioning and behavior of the handler, terrain differences, different types of buildings, different footing, different noises and so on. The list is extensive, and each of us should make our own so that we don't forget the items that are important to us.

> Again, aggression is just another form of behavior. The rules of behavior do not go out the window simply because we are dealing with aggression. What has gone out the window is the need for severe corrections on a frequent basis.

As with other techniques, a small number of dogs learn the behavior well and then just stop doing it. This will be minimized if the proper balance of rewards and corrections is maintained throughout each module, or link in the chain. It may be necessary to administer a reasonable punishment occasionally but the dog should be highly rewarded when it finally complies. This is no different than in other types of training where we need an occasional correction. Again, aggression is just another form of behavior. The rules of behavior do not go out the window simply because we are dealing with aggression. What has gone out the window is the need for severe corrections on a frequent basis. The punishments applied should be reasonable and not needed very often, if at all.

To do this without dropping sleeves trainers can adopt the adaptation used by John Brannon. In this variation of the technique, the handler begins with obedience using toys as the reward. The handler moves to a variable reward schedule as soon as possible (this is where he or she does not reward the dog every time it does something correctly, but randomly so that the dog doesn't need the toy every time and can't predict when it will be given again). When the dog is performing consistently the handler begins to proof the dog off the toys. This begins with the false start. The dog is in a heel position and the toy is thrown but the dog is not released to chase it.

When the dog holds position, it is rewarded with a second toy from the handler. When the dog is performing well on this, it can progress to the recall where the toy is thrown, the dog is released to chase it but then is recalled and must stop chasing the toy and return to the handler. The long line may be used here, but gently, with the handler running along with the dog using the line only to smoothly slow the dog down. At this point the "here" from a distance is also taught. The dog should now be doing consistent off leash obedience with toys thrown all over the ground. This is creating a clear concept in the dog's mind that everything comes from or is withheld by the handler and that this is normal. This will be a great advantage later when severe distractions are encountered. The dog is not allowed to start or terminate a behavior without the handler's approval.

When the obedience is at least 80% efficient, the handler combines it with tug play. First the dog is allowed to play with and win the tug toy. Next the handler produces a second tug toy and trades the dog for the original tug (*figures 5.1, 5.2,* and *5.3*). This begins what is known as the "trade game". It is not usually a problem since the original tug is not moving (it is "dead") and the second tug is being wiggled and moved by the handler (it is "alive"). The dog can then be proofed off all toys and distractions so it focuses on what the handler offers and nothing else (*figure 5.4*). The next step is to have the dog release the tug during a game of tug of war and let it re-bite the same tug as its reward. After the dog is doing this well with the handler, the dog plays the game with someone other than the handler. As the dog progresses the handler varies his distance and location so that the dog doesn't care where the handler is or how far away he may be.

The topic of slipping or dropping sleeves is a controversial one and will probably remain so for some time. The method described above can be used without ever dropping a sleeve and is well suited to trainers who are not in favor of sleeve dropping.

Fig 5.1

fig 5.1· The handler playing tug-of-war with one hand while producing a second tug toy with the other. *Photo by Lisa Brannon.*

At this point the dog is comfortable working for toys, has never been allowed to refuse the handler in anything, is proofed off of toys so it will not be looking for them at inappropriate times, and is comfortable trading a stationary or moving tug toy for either a second tug or a re-bite of the same one. The foundations have now been laid to play the trade game for a man (*figures 5.5* and *5.6*). Note that it could be done with sleeve drops or without ever dropping a sleeve, as the trainer desires. It could be done in a bite suit or without; it is a flexible technique. Work slowly in small increments, and do not be content until you have a dog that will ignore toys, sleeves, suits and anything else you can think of (*figures 5.7, 5.8, 5.9,* and *5.10*) in order to pursue a man. Eventually, the dog will be able to start a pursuit with a tug toy in its mouth, pursue the decoy at full speed past

Fig 5.2

Fig 5.2 · The handler presenting a second tug.
Photo by Lisa Brannon.

multiple tugs on the ground, and bite the decoy with full intensity even though the decoy has been tossing more tugs at the dog as it approaches.

No method is magic, and none will work perfectly on all dogs. The above method has proven itself with good dogs under the guidance of a good trainer, and is offered as a starting point if you have never used this type of training. If your dogs need something slightly different, hang on to the basic principles and adjust the details of what you are doing to suit the animals you have.

The topic of slipping or dropping sleeves is a controversial one and will probably remain so for some time. The method described above can be used without ever dropping a sleeve and is well suited to trainers who are not in favor of sleeve dropping. Those trainers

Fig 5.3

Fig 5.3 · The handler giving the dog a second tug in trade for the first one.
Photo by Lisa Brannon.

who like to drop sleeves may prefer the variation used by Bill Nott. Instead of trading a tug for another tug, the sleeve is dropped first, and after the dog carries it around for a while, it trades the sleeve for a tug toy. The process begins with obedience using some other toy than a tug, saving the tug for bite work. When bite work begins, each session starts with tolerance drills. These are drills in which the dog is expected to stay calm with the decoy behaving in a loud boisterous manner. If obedience has been done properly as described in *Chapter 2*, the dog should be well prepared for this. When the dog remains calm even when tempted and the handler can give all types of announcements and challenges, the dog is rewarded with a tug toy. When the dog is down and quiet, the bite drill can begin. When the dog has a good full mouth bite, the sleeve is slipped and the dog is

Fig 5.4

Fig 5.4 · The dog focusing only on the handler and what he offers.
Photo by Lisa Brannon.

allowed to carry it around for a while. Then the handler produces a tug which he makes more interesting than the motionless sleeve by wiggling and moving it around until the dog drops the sleeve and takes the tug (see figures *5.11, 5.12, 5.13, 5.14,* and *5.15*). This type of "transfer" (from the sleeve to the tug) is performed after the bite three times, and on the third time every person present gathers to let the dog carry its prize (the tug) around through the crowd and

> When bite work begins, each session starts with tolerance drills. These are drills where the dog is expected to stay calm with the decoy behaving in a loud boisterous manner.

everyone makes a big fuss over the dog and lets it show off. The handler never takes the sleeve or the tug from the dog. The dog never

Fig 5.5

Fig 5.5 · The dog should attack with full intensity and bite well.
Photo by Lisa Brannon.

loses anything, and no avoidance behavior develops. Before the dog gets into the car it must release the tug for a different toy (not a tug) signifying that the tug game is over. Remember not to force the issue, be patient.

The next step is to move the handler back and allow the dog to work in front of the handler. After each bite and transfer, the handler returns the sleeve to the decoy and puts it back on him. The decoy is never allowed to take the sleeve back or to try to steal the sleeve from the dog. Competition between the dog and the decoy is not helpful at this point in training, since we are trying to get the dog to give the sleeve up voluntarily. When done properly, the dog will soon begin looking for the tug while it is still carrying the sleeve, anticipating and enjoying the transfer. It is then time to move to the next phase.

Fig 5.6 · The dog trading the decoy for its tug and a game with the handler.
Photo by Lisa Brannon.

The next phase continues the tolerance drills with increased intensity, until the decoy can stand directly in front of the dog screaming and moving and the dog will not bite until given a command. If it will then bite well and transfer from the sleeve to a tug without difficulty, it is time to move on again.

After each bite and transfer the handler returns the sleeve to the decoy and puts it back on him. The decoy is never allowed to take the sleeve back or to try to steal the sleeve from the dog. Competition between the dog and the decoy is not helpful at this point in training since we are trying to get the dog to give the sleeve up voluntarily.

Positioning is the next item to work on. Place a decoy in the centre of an area and pretend the decoy is standing on the centre

Fig 5.7

Fig 5.7 · The dog is ignoring toys, tugs, and suits to focus on a back bite.
Photo by Lisa Brannon.

of a round clock face. The dog is placed in a down on one of the hour number positions and the handler moves to another hour position. He then calls the dog to his new position or downs it anywhere along the way.

By mixing up the sequences in this, the handler gains great control in positioning the dog during drills and real encounters. If obedience has been properly taught as described in *Chapter 2*, the dog will be well prepared for this.

The recall comes next. This begins with a baby recall in which the decoy jogs off with a tug a few steps, stops, and turns to face the dog. The dog downs, with help from the handler if necessary, and the decoy throws the tug over the dog's head (so it has to turn away from the decoy) and the handler plays with the dog. The distance is

Fig 5.8

Fig 5.8 · The dog preparing to engage the decoy. Note toys, sleeves, and bite suits on the ground, as well as tugs tied to and carried by the decoy.
Photo by Lisa Brannon.

increased (using long lines) to at least fifty feet, and tolerance drills are continued throughout the phases. Now the decoy is given a sleeve, and when the dog downs on the recall he comes to the dog for a bite, which still results in a sleeve drop and transfer to a tug.

> Dogs are famous for anticipating the next task in a sequence and jumping to the next step even before it is time to do so. This tendency works in our favor for once.

Lastly, the dog needs to "transfer" off of a sleeve that just happens to be on a man's arm, but it is well prepared to do so.

Dogs are famous for anticipating the next task in a sequence and jumping to the next step even before it is time to do so. This tendency works in our favor for once. For some time now, the dog has been looking for the tug while carrying the sleeve, and when the sleeve stays on the decoy's arm, it is quite willing to cheat and jump to the next step and transfer off the man to the tug (see *figures 5.15. 5.16, 5.17, 5.18, 5.19, and 5.20*). Naturally, this requires a competent decoy who knows enough not to stimulate the dog when it is time to transfer (or just before), but a good decoy is a requirement for all training styles.

Variety is important once the dog understands the drill, and rewards are only given on a random or intermittent schedule, so the handler does not need to have the reward with him all the time and doesn't need to actually use the primary reward in a real situation. Training is not complete until the

Fig 5.9

Fig 5.9 · The dog ignores the proofing materials as the decoy presents himself for an inside arm bite.
Photo by Lisa Brannon.

Fig 5.10

Fig 5.10 · The dog ignores the tugs tied to and carried by the decoy and bites the man hard on the inside of the arm.
Photo by Lisa Brannon.

dog is proofed off of the tug toys.

The above techniques offer great advantages over the older, more compulsive techniques, but there are still some ways to mess them up.

For example, if the wrong toy or game is used, it will not create enough motivation in the dog to produce the behavior we want. It is important to take time in the beginning of training to identify the exact toy or game the dog values the most and to make sure that this is what the dog is being offered for its "trade" or "transfer".

Another mistake people are likely to make is that of improperly or incompletely proofing the dog off the toys. Enough dogs have been trained with these techniques now to demonstrate that the use of toys and games do not cause problems in

Fig 5.11

Fig. 5.11 · The dog should pursue the decoy with full intensity.
Photo by John Johnston.

good dogs that have been properly trained. If your finished dogs are looking for toys, examine your canine selection procedures and your proofing abilities.

There are a few dogs out there that have trouble with over-excitability, what is sometimes called "sensory overload". When they get above a certain level of excitement, they cannot think or act in a controlled manner. Sometimes this is a result of a traumatic event and

Enough dogs have been trained with these techniques now to demonstrate that the use of toys and games do not cause problems in good dogs which have been properly trained. If your finished dogs are looking for toys, examine your canine selection procedures and your proofing abilities.

Fig 5.12

Fig. 5.12 · The dog should commit fully to a good bite.
Photo by John Johnston.

sometimes it is just the natural condition for the dog, so in some animals it is a temporary condition, and with some it is a lifelong problem. Regardless of its duration or cause, these animals must be treated in a dull, boring manner in order to keep their excitement at levels where they can perform well (see *Chapter 1* on the Yerkes-Dodson law). The pain of a punishment creates excitement in the dog and needs to be avoided for training to progress.

Most of the techniques described in this book will provide aggression control without using pain as the primary tool. The interesting thing here is that a good game with the right toy is also exciting and can in itself cause a loss of control. It doesn't matter to these dogs what the source of excitement is, pain or pleasure, they can't handle either. Both are exciting, and it is the excitement itself

Fig. 5.13 · The decoy slipping the sleeve after the handler has the short lead.
Photo by John Johnston.

that causes lack of control. So with these dogs we must avoid games and toys as well as pain until they gain the ability to handle excitement. If you are dealing with a dog that has a genetic disposition for this problem, it will not gain this ability. You are more likely to see this type of dog now than you were years ago since we are experiencing an industry wide problem with recognizing the difference between high levels of motivation and wildness. A highly motivated dog has high levels of

In a desire to obtain an energetic dog, some trainers are accepting dogs that have high energy levels but have no focus and lose the ability to reason when they begin to work. This is simply wildness and has no place in police work. Police dogs need to be able to think in order to solve problems in their every day work.

Fig 5.14

Fig. 5.14 · The dog transfers to the tug toy after carrying the sleeve for a while.
Photo by John Johnston.

energy in its approach to work but the energy is focused and the dog is able to think at all times. In a desire to obtain an energetic dog, some trainers are accepting dogs that have high energy levels but have no focus and lose the ability to reason when they begin to work. This is simply wildness, and has no place in police work. Police dogs need to be able to think in order to solve problems in their every day work.

This is one of the major differences between police and other dogs, and we must not allow it to be forgotten or passed over. Unbalanced wild dogs are not what we should be looking for or demanding from our suppliers. However this is a discussion for another time and place, so let us conclude by saying that if you are unfortunate enough to have to train such a dog, keep everything dull and boring so as to

Fig 5.15

Fig. 5.15 · Transfer complete.
Photo by John Johnston.

keep the dog at a reasonable level of excitement and you will have much greater success.

Some dogs get dirty and start cheating after they get their first actual bite in the real world. This is a minor problem with dogs trained in the above manner, since they already know what the correct behavior is, and a small number of standard corrections straighten them out and are often unnecessary thereafter. Abusive levels of pain are not required. Remember that behaviors which are taught with positive reinforcement techniques last longer and are generally more reliable than those taught with punishment.

Behaviorists have long known that punishment is a temporary tool, and unless it is completely traumatic its effects do not last long. This is why most dogs need to be "cleaned up" on a regular basis,

Fig 5.16

Fig. 5.16 · Full intensity pursuit. Good dogs do not look for toys.
Photo by John Johnston.

since they were trained with punishment as the major training tool. Using positive reinforcement really pays off now, since the dogs are more willing to return to the behaviors we want, and its effects last much longer.

CASE EXAMPLE: The scene was a national training workshop in North Carolina in the month of June. The weather was hot and humid, as you might imagine. In fact, everything was as you would imagine, except that one of the instructors in aggression control was teaching the use of toys and games as a reward for the release after the bite. Since this was a rare occurrence at the time, it attracted a certain amount of attention, even from handlers who were merely observing and had not brought their dogs. One of these handlers worked for

Fig 5.17

Fig. 5.17 · Good dogs still use hard, full mouth bites with these techniques.
Photo by John Johnston.

a rural Sheriff's office, and had been watching other people's dogs working for some time without saying a word. Finally, he approached the instructor and asked if he would still be around in another hour. Apparently he wanted to drive home and return with his dog, but did not want to return and find the instructor gone. The instructor assured him he would remain on the field until the handler returned and work resumed on other dogs.

Sure enough, an hour later the handler returned and introduced the instructor to Rex (not his real name). Rex was a young, medium sized male German Shepherd Dog. He was sable in color and his story was a familiar one. He performed well in everything else, but had never outed properly, even in basic school. No amount of compulsion seemed to be enough to change his mind, and the handler eventually

Fig 5.18

Fig. 5.18 · The dog anticipating the transfer, except this time the sleeve is on the man. *Photo by John Johnston.*

resigned himself to the fact that he would have to have to work this dog carefully, and hope that he would never have to call him off anyone. The handler developed the habit of not bringing Rex to seminars, but when he saw the positive results the instructor was getting with everyone else's dogs, he decided to give this new approach a try. The instructor asked the handler to get Rex's favorite toy, so he went back to his vehicle, took out a common tennis ball and returned. Rex was given a bite and the handler was positioned so that Rex could see both the decoy and the handler. The decoy kept the excitement to a minimum and when the handler showed the tennis ball and gave the out command, Rex popped right off the sleeve the very first time and returned to the handler, who immediately gave him his favorite game. As with many dogs, Rex had never wanted to

Fig 5.19

Fig 5.19 · The dog completes the transfer to the tug.
Photo by John Johnston.

be a problem; he simply had not been set up properly to succeed and had never been offered a decent substitute for the decoy. When he was given a chance, he turned out to be no problem at all. These techniques do not always work as quickly as they did in Rex's case, but they often do, and Rex's story is not too unusual

SECOND CASE EXAMPLE: Ruger (not his real name) was a large, black male German Shepherd Dog who had always been a problem in aggression control. He had an excellent trainer and good decoys, but had always required heavy doses of electricity to work, and even then things were difficult. When he knew electricity was coming, he would stiffen his neck, scream, and bite harder instead of releasing. Only the most massive amounts of electricity would convince Ruger to be

Fig. 5.20 · The end result: after a pursuit and bite, the handler calls the dog out from a distance while he stays under cover.
Photo by John Johnston.

compliant, he was never really reliable, and the trainer was never really happy with the situation. After much discussion, the trainer decided to give toys and games a try, since compulsion was not yielding the results he wanted. It was decided to use a variation of the sleeve transfer method with four different sleeves. The sleeves were placed in separate locations. The decoy put on the first sleeve and gave the dog a bite. The sleeve was slipped, and Ruger was allowed to carry the sleeve around. During this time, the decoy slowly moved to the second location and put on the second sleeve. The handler then brought Ruger over and positioned him in front of the decoy and waited for the dog to drop the first sleeve which was still in his mouth. As soon as Ruger dropped the first sleeve, he was immediately given a bite with the second sleeve, and allowed to carry it around when it too was slipped. During this time, the decoy moved to the third sleeve and put it on. The handler positioned Ruger in front of the decoy again, and when the dog dropped the second sleeve he was immediately given a bite with the third sleeve, which was slipped so he could carry it around also. After Ruger was transferred to the fourth sleeve in a similar manner and allowed to carry it around, he was transferred off the sleeve to a tug in the normal manner and the session was over. Ruger began to anticipate and enjoy the transfers and, after three sessions with the four sleeves, was outing normally off the man with no sleeve slipping and no electricity.

Chapter 6
Problem Solving

There are many complications to teaching the dog to release after the bite, but some are seen more frequently than others. Among these would be: starting with a dog which is too wild for this kind of work in the first place; not preparing the dog properly during obedience; having a decoy who places the dog in the wrong part of the inverted U (see *Chapter 1* on the Yerkes-Dodson law); using equipment which overexcites the dog; and having a competitive relationship between the dog and the handler. While these are all seen frequently, by far the most commonly seen problem is that of using too much pain and punishment in the process. This book is an attempt to emphasize techniques which avoid this problem by minimizing or completely eliminating the need for pain and punishment during the teaching process. Keep in mind that the rules of operant conditioning do not go out the window simply because we are dealing with aggression. All the rules of behavioral science are still in effect, and if they work on animals like killer whales (which they do) they will certainly work on aggressive dogs.

Although the self out, game playing, and the use of toys work best on untrained dogs in initial training, they were not originally designed for green dogs. When they were first developed by the author in the late 1970s and early 1980s they were created for dogs with control problems. Most of these were dogs that reacted badly to severe punishments, which at that time were routinely used for teaching control. It was only later that trainers realized how effective these techniques are with green dogs.

Dog trainers have had good success over the years with problem behaviors by identifying and eliminating the triggers (the stimuli which cause an animal to exhibit a certain behavior) and the reinforcers. This allows the problem behavior to extinguish (disappear) and lets the trainers reinforce or reward a behavior that is more to their liking. In aggression control, pain is often the trigger for our problems. In many cases, simply eliminating pain as the major teaching tool significantly improves the situation.

> Dogs with high pain tolerances can survive severe punishments, and learn to compete with and fight against the handler. This encourages them to cheat during aggression control in order to beat the handler and get what they want.
> In many cases, the roots of this entire problem are both the severe punishment and the dog's reaction to the pain.

The type of dog we select for aggression work is not the kind of animal that gives up easily. When confronted with a problem, a good candidate dog will keep working to solve it. If the problem is a handler who is being unreasonable, the dog will keep working to solve this problem as well, even when severe punishments are involved. Dogs with high pain tolerances can survive severe punishments, and learn to compete with and fight against the handler. This encourages them to cheat during aggression control in order to beat the handler and get what they want.

In many cases, the roots of this entire problem are both the severe punishment and the dog's reaction to the pain. What if we remove pain from the process entirely? The dog would have nothing to react badly to, and every behavior that is a result of the bad reaction would disappear. This is the basis of the self out, game playing and using toys. When we avoid the bad reactions to severe punishment, training becomes more effective. Add to this a good relationship with the handler, established during obedience (see *Chapter 2*), and teaching aggression control becomes much easier. The quality of the dog's life also improves. Most of the tough, well bred dogs that are selected for working purposes are quite intelligent for their species. They do not need severe punishments to learn and enjoy their jobs. Give them a competent leader who does not abuse them and they will learn aggression control easily, and perform at levels that will astound most people. Start a fight with them and you have a substantial enemy to deal with. Most will fight you to the bitter end. In many cases, they are better fighters than we are, and we lose. We end up with a resentful, contentious dog that cheats at every opportunity. Fortunately, this is not necessary, and can be completely avoided by following the advice in this book. By using the techniques described in the previous chapters, you can have a dog that learns quickly, performs reliably, respects its leader and enjoys life. It's a good deal.

The techniques described in this book often work quite quickly, but with some dogs they require more repetitions. When dealing with problem behaviors, we should be cautious of quick fixes. What we want is a long lasting change, not a partial fix that appears quickly but fades away just as fast. This quick fading is often what we get when we use punishment as the major training tool. As stated before, punishment is a temporary tool, and its results do not last long unless some form of trauma is involved. This explains the large number of dogs that need to be re-trained or "cleaned up" frequently, since punishment was a major part of their training for control. Behaviors created and reinforced positively usually show better reliability and longevity, and we have definitely seen this in aggression control work. Unfortunately, trainers who want to use the techniques described in this book are often put under time pressure. They are frequently at seminars with only a short time frame to work with when presented with problem dogs and everyone wants them to fix the problems in a day or two. What everyone forgets is that it took many repetitions to create the problems, and it may take more than just a few repetitions of good techniques to counteract them in any meaningful way.

A quick fix is easier to accomplish in a short time frame, and this is what most trainers choose to do. We need to encourage trainers to demonstrate good, long lasting techniques and let someone else finish the work when they go home, rather than pressuring them mentally to give us a quick fix that will get us through certification but will fade quickly when we return home. One of the most important lessons for new trainers is to make time to do things correctly rather than messing things up by trying to take shortcuts.

As mentioned above, pain induced aggression plays a major part in many of the problems we face in aggression control. This is a type of aggression whose biological purpose is to increase the survivability of the dog by making pain go away. Pain is a biological warning system which gets the dog's attention and signals that something is wrong and needs to be taken care of immediately. Consequently, making pain disappear often improves the dog's condition and increases its chances of survival. When dogs with a genetic predisposition for this type of aggression feel pain, they attack what they perceive to be the source. If they think that this aggression helps their cause or actually makes the pain go away, they will repeat the behavior with greater intensity the next time they experience pain. This is the basis of the old, out dated agitation techniques of flanking, pinching, whipping the front legs with sticks and feeding dogs gunpowder. These techniques created aggression, but also created side effects that caused many safety problems for the people who had to live with or service the dogs. Fortunately, we now have better ways to stimulate aggression humanely, and do not need to use these old techniques any longer. As stated before, pain induced aggression has a genetic predisposition and is quite prevalent in dogs. It is one reason that all working dogs should be trained to be comfortable in a non-restrictive agitation type muzzle. Then, when they are injured, we can muzzle them as a first step without increasing their stress levels. We are then safe to handle and help them without getting bitten in the process.

Getting back to using pain in aggression control work, it hardly makes sense to use a tool that will increase aggression at a time when we are trying to teach the dog to lower its aggression levels. It makes more sense to avoid tools that increase aggression when we are trying to teach control.

The only reason that pain ever works in aggression control is that if you create a high enough level of pain, you will produce what is known as an "escape reaction". This is a situation where the pain is so great that it surpasses the dog's pain tolerance. The stimulation is so unpleasant that the dog decides that it must stop everything it is doing in order to escape from the pain. It therefore stops being aggressive and finds other things to do. This was an effective technique for many years, until we started getting dogs in training that had higher pain tolerances. As the dogs exhibited higher and higher pain tolerances, we found it more and more difficult to get a good enough punishment applied to the dog. It was more and more difficult to create an escape reaction when we needed it. We had to start using pinch collars instead of standard training collars. Then the pinch collar didn't work well enough and we had to move up to double pinch collars. Then came the third party correction, sometimes with double pinch collars, and finally electricity. As the pain tolerances got higher, we got into more and more trouble, until now it is not difficult to find dogs that anticipate the release command, tighten their necks, scream, and bite harder the more pain is inflicted upon them. These dogs have such high pain tolerances that it is no longer effective for us to rely upon the escape reaction. It is time for us to adjust. Actually, it is way past time. The first step to adjusting is to consider and study techniques which minimize the use of pain.

The other form of aggression that complicates control work is what is known as redirected aggression. This is aggression that has been diverted from its preferred target to a secondary target (hence the name "redirected"). When the dog is biting the decoy it is doing what it has been trained to do, what it considers to be proper. When the handler starts using pain during this process (in an attempt to get the dog to stop biting) this is annoying, since the dog is only doing what it has been trained to do. Many dogs would like to bite the handler at this point, but it is against the rules of the dog world to bite an upper ranking animal. The aggression has to go somewhere so the dog looks around for some other target. There is only one lower ranking animal close at hand to release this aggression on: the decoy. So the dog bites harder. By using pain we have guaranteed that the dog will not lower its aggression level but in fact will bite harder the more pain we inflict on it. Unless we achieve an escape reaction the dog will simply bite harder and harder and it is our fault.

> Many of these dogs are not trying to be difficult; they are simply being forced into bad behavior by poorly educated humans.

So whether we are dealing with pain induced aggression or redirected aggression, the use of pain simply raises the aggression levels and works against us. Many of these dogs are not trying to be difficult; they are simply being forced into bad behavior by poorly educated humans. Different dogs have different genetic predispositions towards these problems so we will not always see them, but many problem dogs are wrestling with these issues. By using the techniques listed in this book you give these animals the maximum chance of improving. You will improve the quality of their lives at the same time. If you feel a responsibility to your dogs, you can express that by becoming skillful with less painful training techniques.

Many dogs improve faster if you change the commands you use for the release and control. The old commands are sounds that seem to carry old memories and trigger old responses. These old responses are the reason the dog has been brought to you so we need to leave them behind. Using a different system of training with different commands seems to help many dogs make the transition more easily.

Sometimes the techniques we are using are not well suited to the breed of dog we are working with, and we need to improve them. Many trainers begin their careers working with the German Shepherd Dog (for good reason), and develop habits and preferences which fit this particular breed quite well.

However, some of these habits do not fit other breeds quite as well as they do the German Shepherd Dog. When we try to force these other breeds into the mold of the German Shepherd Dog, we can get in trouble. Most German Shepherds are reasonable animals, so we can bully them into doing things if we are consistent about how we do it. This is not good training for the breed, but we get away with it because of their particular genetic background. The dog will eventually figure out what we want, and has a basic desire to work with its leader. Other breeds have different genetic backgrounds, and do not show this behavior as strongly as the German Shepherd Dog. Two cases in point are the Rottweiler and the Belgian Malinois. When these breeds first became popular in the United States, we got into trouble with them because we insisted that they behave like the German Shepherd Dog. When we used techniques designed to force the German Shepherd Dog into compliance, the new breeds fought back. Most experienced trainers will agree that if you start fights with Rottweilers or Belgian Malinois, many of them will fight you to the death just out of principle. In an effort to evade responsibility for using poor training techniques, many people tried to blame the dogs by labeling them as "stubborn" when actually they were not stubborn at all. If we take the time to motivate them properly with positive techniques, they are not at all difficult to work with. They simply won't be bullied into things, especially by pain.

> Sometimes the techniques we are using are not well suited to the breed of dog we are working with and we need to improve them.

When you are having trouble teaching the dog to release the decoy, it might be helpful to go through the following list of items and discuss them with other experienced trainers:

1) Is the dog in the top of the inverted U? Have you commanded the dog at the correct time? Can the dog think clearly? Make sure you control the dog's excitement levels properly. Refer to *Chapter 1* on the Yerkes-Dodson Law. Examine all possible sources of excitement.

2) What have you done in obedience to prepare the dog for this? Refer to *Chapter 2,* and remember that a dog who will not release a toy is not ready to release a man.

3) Have you taught the dog, or are you bullying him with pain? Have you gone back to the beginning of the teaching process? Are you sure the dog understands what you want?

4) Are you fighting old memories? If the dog has previous training experience, have you changed the type of location, decoys, equipment, training sequences, commands, and even the language?

5) Are your techniques well suited to the particular breed of dog you are working with? Are you trying to force some other breed of dog to act like a German Shepherd Dog?

6) Is the dog competing with the handler? This often starts in obedience, so review *Chapter 2* and go back and re-teach if necessary. Look for any tendency of the dog to spin the decoy to get away from the handler.

7) Is the handler doing his/her job correctly? Is he/she using the correct sequences at the proper time? Is he/she distracting, threatening the dog, or creating aggression or confusion?

8) Is the decoy doing his/her job correctly? Is he/she using submissive signals? Is he/she keeping the dog's excitement levels in the proper range? Is he/she keeping the dog between the decoy and the handler?

9) Are the handler and the decoy synchronized? Are they both asking for the same thing at the same time?

10) What is rewarding the bad behavior? If a behavior (even a bad behavior) exists, it is being rewarded, so search for the reward and eliminate it.

11) How can you increase the reward for releasing? If a behavior (even a good behavior) does not exist, the dog is not anticipating a sufficient reward, so increase the reward and find a way to get the dog to think it is coming right after the release.

12) Have you set any patterns with locations, sequences, decoys, equipment etc., that are hurting the process?

13) Have you tried the muzzle? Don't give up till you have. Remember that with any behavior, when the teeth are part of the problem, sometimes the muzzle is part of the solution.

14) As with all problem solving, when everything logical fails, try something illogical (as long as it is humane – this is not to be used as an excuse for abusive treatment – this is simply just a change of logic).

Returning to the idea of eliminating the triggers and reinforcements of problem behaviors, this book should give you more options than the older methods that are still so popular. As you gain more experience with these techniques you will no doubt add improvements that will increase their effectiveness. This is good as long as we continue to decrease our reliance and dependence upon pain as a teaching tool. We are so much better off now than we were in the old days it is sometimes difficult to comprehend. We should continue this improvement. This book should be only the beginning.

Chapter 7
Decoys and Equipment

The most important tool a trainer has is a good decoy. From the first day of obedience training the decoy should be present, but he/she must behave properly. For the decoy to become a neutral stimulus he/she should be fully dressed as a decoy but acting normally so the dog has no reason to focus on him/her. The concept we are trying to teach the dog is that it is the behavior of the decoy that determines whether or not he/she should be bitten, not the clothes or equipment they are wearing. The lesson will not be complete until aggression training begins, but it begins by showing the dog a non aggressive decoy and rewarding it for behaving normally around him/her.

Decoys makes or break the dog, particularly in sensitive parts of training. They must be skilled communicators, and have good coordination and timing. They must also understand the Yerkes-Dodson law (see *Chapter 1*) and how their actions move the dog along the inverted U. Loading the dog by using exciting movements or signals at the wrong time will destroy everything the trainer is trying to accomplish. For this reason, many trainers learn how to decoy and play the role themselves so as to minimize mistakes. Being the decoy themselves also allows trainers to avoid arguments with their decoy, which is one of the biggest problems trainers can have. For some reason, many decoys reach a stage of development where they feel they know more than the trainer. To become really useful, a decoy must work through this phase of development, but some never make it. They spend the rest of their careers arguing with trainers about what should be done with their dogs. Their physical skills are worthless at this point, since trainers cannot trust them to do what they're told. If you are working with a decoy who will not do exactly what you ask when he/she disagrees with you, it would be better for you to get a new decoy, particularly if his/her actions are placing the dog in the wrong part of the inverted U. Nothing good comes from a decoy exciting the dog at the wrong time.

Decoys should always be using signals that are appropriate to what the trainer is trying to accomplish. This is particularly true than when we are working on the release. If decoys are using challenging signals immediately before or during the time that the handler is giving the release command, they are working against the trainer at a time when they should be helping.

> If you are working with a decoy who will not do exactly as you ask when he/she disagrees with you, it would be better for you to get a new decoy, particularly if his/her actions are placing the dog in the wrong part of the inverted U.

Many dogs are dominating the decoy during the biting process and if the subordinate animal (the decoy) challenges them, it will motivate the dogs to continue biting to maintain or complete their dominance. Challenging signals are appropriate in many phases of training, but decoys should switch to submissive signals when the trainer is teaching the release.

Communication and signaling between the decoy and the dog are discussed in the author's previous book, *Decoys and Aggression: A Police K9 Training Manual*. Only upper ranking animals are allowed to use what are known as "distance increasing" signals. In the world of dogs, these "go away" signals are considered to be challenging, and lower ranking animals are not allowed to use them. If they do, it is the job of the upper ranking dog to maintain order in the pack by punishing the offender. Since they often do this by biting, it is not good for the decoy to use these signals when the trainer is trying to encourage the dog to stop biting. To be helpful when the trainer is teaching the release, decoys should avoid distance increasing signals such as quick, exciting movement; facing the dog squarely; direct eye contact, and towering over the dog. They should instead be using the submissive signals of standing still for inspection; rotating their body sideways as much as possible; breaking eye contact, and lowering their body slightly. Decoys should always be flexible and willing to adapt their actions to surprise situations.

Handlers are just as prone to making mistakes as anyone else, especially under pressure. It is possible for handlers to give the wrong commands, or the right commands at the wrong time. Even when these commands are completely contrary to the training plan, no matter how well said plan was discussed, they are still commands and cannot be ignored without consequence. It is the job of the decoy to support the handler's commands with the appropriate actions and let the trainer deal with the consequences. The actions of the decoy and the handler should always be synchronized, and hopefully the handler will get better at following the trainer's directions. Again, handlers are the trainer's responsibility, not the decoy's. The decoy's job is to synchronize with the handler, unless the trainer gives him/her direct orders to the contrary.

How the decoy positions the dog is an important item. As we know from obedience, dogs think differently when the handler is either out of range or somehow physically blocked from reaching them. We seem to get better behavior when they realize that the handler has direct access to them. This is particularly true when the dog has a competitive relationship with the handler. Dogs who like to cheat or compete with the handler tend to do so more when they are out of the handler's reach than when they know the handler can touch them. During bite work, this leads to dogs spinning the decoy around so that they are on the far side of the decoy when they don't want the handler to interfere with them, such as when they know the release command is coming and they don't want to let go just yet. Any time the dog wants to be independent of the handler during bite work, it will try to spin the decoy around to get away from the handler. So to contribute to success properly, the decoy must keep the dog from spinning him/her and keep it positioned so that it is directly between the decoy and the handler. This gives the handler direct physical access to the dog and encourages the dog to think more cooperatively, since it cannot escape from the reach of the handler. The decoy should always inform the trainer that the dog is trying to get away from the handler since this indicates an improper relationship between the two and that there is some underlying issue that needs to be addressed. It can range anywhere from simple competition to the fact that the dog feels the handler's presence is a threat and is trying to get away from him/her to avoid the bad treatment it has received in the past. Whatever the cause, something needs to be improved but this is a job for the trainer, not the decoy. The decoy's job is merely to inform the trainer of the dog's desire to spin him/her.

> So to contribute to success properly, the decoy must keep the dog from spinning him/her and keep it positioned so that it is directly between the decoy and the handler.

The general relationship between the dog and the decoy can sometimes cause trouble. When sleeve dropping, or slipping the sleeve is used, some trainers encourage the decoy to try to steal the dropped sleeve back from the dog after it has been dropped. This creates a more possessive frame of mind in the dog, and often produces a dog which will fight harder for the sleeve and score higher in competition. While this is an advantage for some sport dogs, it creates a strongly competitive relationship between the dog and the decoy that can cause problems when the dog is expected to release. Generally, it is not an advantage to have a dog obsessively fighting for possession of the sleeve when we are trying to teach the out. It is a time when we want the dog to give up the sleeve and stop competing with the decoy. If you have spent a great deal of time setting up too much competition and desire for the sleeve in the dog, it will really hurt you when it comes time to teach the out. For this reason, many trainers are moving away from the old techniques where the sleeve is left on the ground in front of the dog and the decoy tries to steal it back from the dog. They now look ahead and plan for the day when they will have to teach the release; and when they do things go much better.

Sometimes it is an advantage to switch equipment. Some dogs have a habit of getting their teeth caught in the sleeve or bite suit and cannot release even when they choose to. This often happens when the material is worn-out and frayed. Occasionally, all you have to do is use better equipment to help the dog learn what you are trying to teach. In other cases, dogs may be more willing to release when they are working on hard hidden sleeves than when you are using soft jute material. Old memories can also cause complications. If the dog's previous trainer expected wild, undisciplined behavior when a certain piece of equipment was used, the dog may not understand that you expect something different in the presence of that same equipment. This often occurs with regard to the bite suit. Since people feel a little safer when using one, they frequently encourage the dog to be little wilder when using one. Sometimes this complicates the teaching of the release since the mere presence of a bite suit excites the dog more than any other type of equipment. The muzzle can have this same effect if it is only used during aggression work. Whenever you get the impression that the dog is trying to release but is having difficulty, it is worth your while to switch the type of equipment you are using

> Occasionally all you have to do is use better equipment to help the dog learn what you are trying to teach.

before you give up. Also, check your dog to make sure it will release off of all different types of equipment. If you only use certain types of equipment when teaching the release, the dog may not realize that you want it to release off other types. Dogs that generalize well will have no problems, but those that discriminate well can suffer confusion when you set a pattern regarding equipment or even the decoys themselves.

> Whenever you get the impression that the dog is trying to release but is having difficulty, it is worth your while to switch the type of equipment you are using before you give up.

In essence, decoys must be physically skilled, good at positioning, good communicators, and willing to follow instructions, even when they disagree with the trainer. If they are not, your dogs will have difficulty learning aggression control. If you do not have a good decoy make searching for one a top priority. Good decoys are worth their weight in gold.

CASE EXAMPLE: Shep (not his real name) was a German Shepherd Dog who began his life in Europe as a working dog candidate, and relatively little is known or remembered of him before he was selected by an importer and flown to the United States. Like hundreds of dogs before him, Shep was examined by several people, most of whom recognized that he had all the necessary qualities to become a good police dog.

Eventually he found himself enrolled in a basic patrol dog school of the K9 unit of a large city on the east coast. His handler was as talented as most new handlers, and while no K9 team is ever perfect, they posed no great problems as they progressed through school and were soon graduated and put to work on the streets of the city.

Everything was going fine until at some point they were forced to physically engage a very large male suspect who was clearly committed to resisting arrest. The suspect was inside a room, and as soon as Shep made contact, the suspect turned his attention to the dog, and the fight was on. More than once during the prolonged fight, Shep was thrown through the air to smash against the nearest wall and slide down to the floor; more than once Shep picked himself up and hurled himself back into the fight. Many dogs would have quit under this kind of stress, but his genetics were good, he was well raised and trained, and he was not about to give up easily. Eventually, the suspect was subdued and taken into custody.

Shep had performed magnificently and was a complete credit to his breeder, his importer, his trainer and his handler; but he was never the same again. The stress and trauma of the event had changed the way he thought and related to people and the world in general. He became unpredictable (except for the fact that he would not release a decoy) and was so dangerous to be around that the city was forced to consider taking him off the street, which would have been more than the loss of a good dog; it would have been the loss of a great deal of time and money as well.

The author knew that something was outside the normal when he was asked to evaluate Shep, because the trainer was one of the best in the business and did not need help to train a dog. So it was time to focus on the decoys to see how they fit into the equation. It was soon evident that changing the behavior of the decoys might help. They were working Shep in the same manner they had before the fight, whereas his needs had changed. What used to be a healthy amount of stimulation was now too much for him, and was pushing him over the top of the Inverted U into the right side where performance deteriorates (see *Chapter 1* on the Yerkes-Dodson Law).

Shep's enemy was excitement, and the only people who could help him were his decoys. Once the trainer realized this, he changed the decoy's routines to incorporate slower movements, less challenging signals, and no fighting during the bite itself, making bitework quite boring. However, this held Shep's excitement down to a level at which the dog could think, and he began to learn that he was still capable of handling difficult situations. As Shep's confidence in his own abilities began to rise back to where it had been before the fight, his behavior became more confident and predictable, with the added benefit that he began to release decoys again. The boring behavior of the decoys shifted the dog to the left on the Inverted U, and his performance rose back to previous levels. As time passed, the decoys found they could shift their behavior back to normal and, as long as they didn't do anything too wild, Shep continued to out off the bad guy.

While it is not always possible to reclaim dogs after bad experiences, the decoys are often a critical element in the process. In this case, they helped a good dog overcome the effects of a traumatic experience, and saved their city a lot of money at the same time.